Sex and the Christian Life

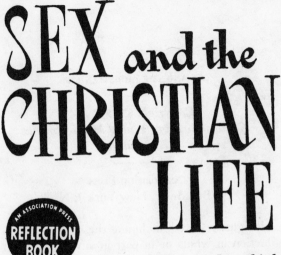

SEX and the CHRISTIAN LIFE

An Association Press
REFLECTION BOOK

In which

SEWARD HILTNER

draws from his SEX ETHICS

AND THE KINSEY REPORTS

Association Press • New York

SEX AND THE CHRISTIAN LIFE

*Copyright © 1957 by
National Board of Young Men's Christian
Associations*

Association Press
291 Broadway, New York 7, N. Y.

*Library of Congress catalog card
number: 57-11607*

Printed in the United States of America

Contents

Introduction

From the Christian point of view, sex is intended by God to occupy a positive and significant place in the life of mankind. Sex interest, activity, and expression are not in themselves mere concessions to human weakness. Men and women may indeed be a little lower than the angels. Lower or not, the nature of our creaturehood is certainly different from theirs, and God made it so.

When a man or woman becomes a Christian, he is, in the traditional language, a "new being in Jesus Christ." This new creature is then no longer under the sway of the "old Adam." He becomes aware of his salvation and redemption through the love of God revealed by Jesus Christ.

What this means, in more modern terminology, is that becoming a Christian changes the central focus of life. There is a new perspective from which all of life is examined. Life and one's self still contain the same details, tasks, troubles, and potentialities they had before. Man's new being in Christ does not eliminate personal problems nor make him sinless. Instead, it gives him another focus on his problems and fresh courage to tackle them. It enables him to receive God's forgiveness for his sin, and there is a consequent healing of the breach between himself and God that is the essence of sin. He lives the Christian life in a continuingly imperfect world, no more perfect or errorless than he was before—but with a view of God and a faith in God which alters the meaning of all that he feels, thinks, and does.

As a new creature, just as in the old Adam, he still has sex as a dimension of his life. What may be new is the way he views it, his total attitude or feeling toward its place and function. Perhaps before he had regarded sex as an instrument for the

exploitation of others to his own pleasure.
Now he sees such a view as negative, as destroying all the possibilities for mutuality
that are inherent in the full dimensions of
human sex life. Or perhaps previously he
had viewed sex as something contaminated,
to be kept as far away as possible. Now he
understands that in God's view, there is
nothing inferior or dirty about sex or about
the body; that positive acceptance of himself as a total spirit includes acceptance of
his sexuality and a right use of it. What his
faith does is to provide a new focus, a new
perspective, a new basis for evaluation.

These truths may indeed be self-evident
in relation to many realms of life. Now in
the Christian faith, endeavoring to live the
Christian life, one still earns a living, cares
for his children, pursues hobbies, enjoys
time with his friends, gives some service to
his community—but these efforts are re-
valued and re-examined with his new focus.
They may be more necessary, more positive,

or more important than he ever felt them to be before. The same is true of sex, but, for many complex reasons, a similar conclusion has not always been drawn about sex, as it should be.

The fact is that many good Christians, well aware that their faith has implications for every dimension of life, have not, however, thought through the meaning of this faith in relation to sex. The late Alfred C. Kinsey conducted many thousands of interviews with people, many of them Christians, about the detailed facts of their sexual behavior. So many of them indicated to him that their faith had a purely "reproductive" view of sex (that sex activity is justified *only* by a reproductive end or aim) that Kinsey concluded this was normative for the relation between sex and the Christian life. As a matter of fact, any such view is false to the biblical message and to much of Christian history. If it is prominent in our day, then we need two things: an exposure of such a view as being out of line with the Christian witness, and a re-examination of the sources of our faith and their implication for the Christian life. That is the task that lies before us in this volume.

The first, the most basic, and the most authoritative witness to the essential nature of our faith is found in the Bible. We shall, then, examine the way in which the Bible regards sex. We shall find and acknowledge different levels of thinking about sex in the Bible, but we shall also present a central and focal view to which we believe the biblical accounts all point. We shall then study briefly what happened to the biblical view of sex in the two thousand years of Western Christian history. We shall note what seem to be gains in ways of realizing the intention inherent in the biblical view, and also distortions of the basic message that have been and are still at work in Christian thought and life.

Since we believe that significant light has

been shed on the nature and meaning of sex in uniquely human life by many kinds of modern studies—psychoanalysis, the Kinsey studies, and many others—we shall make reference to the way in which these findings are related to the Christian view. In terms of general and comprehensive principles, the attempt will then be made to restate the Christian view of sex in modern terms—based on the biblical view, including the implementations from Christian historical development, and in the light of modern studies involving sex.

Finally, and all too briefly, we shall explore some practical implications of the Christian view of sex. What does all this imply for sex in marriage, for premarriage or extramarriage sexual relationships, for sex for the unmarried, and other related matters? Our discussion will presuppose no automatic or coded answers to such questions, but we believe the answers can be wrought out, by individuals and by the

Christian community, if there is a firm grasp upon the Christian principles and a fearless examination of the facts.

The focus of this book is *sex* and the Christian life. Since sex cannot be discussed without reference to marriage, to love, and to other matters of great importance, these will of course have some mention. But sex itself, if taken in its full human dimensions as Christianity sees them, is worthy of consideration in its own right. It is to this that the book is addressed.

CHAPTER 1

Differing Views of Sex

The place of sex in the Christian life has received a wide variety of answers from Christians. Tertullian, Jerome, and even the great Augustine believed that a holding down of sex impulses was a good thing in itself and pleasing to God, although they recognized that such complete suppression seemed impossible to most people. In contrast, Martin Luther left the monastery and married in order to demonstrate that there was no special religious merit or virtue in suppressing sex.

In the sexual as in other realms of life Christians have often failed to live up to what they believed to be right according to the Christian view. But there is more to the differences than a discrepancy between ideal and conduct. There have also been significant differences in terms of conviction and point of view. In our own land we may think, for instance, of the Mormons whose plural marriage, whatever the complex motivations behind it, insured that every woman was in a responsible family atmosphere in the frontier communities. Or we think of the Oneida community of the early nineteenth century, now perpetuated in memory when a silver chest is given to an engaged daughter, but once an experiment in a marriage system with no permanent ties, undertaken on Christian grounds.

More significant than the differences of conviction among these relatively smaller groups have been those among large groups of Christians: Roman Catholics and Protestants, Italians and British, Greek and Swedish, Oriental and Occidental. No doubt many of the differences between such groups are merely cultural in nature, but every such group, explicitly or implicitly, has claimed a basis for its view not only in its culture but also in its interpretation of Christianity.

How can we account for these convinced diversities? One reason lies in the fact that Christianity did not come into being as a rule book. It came, instead, as a way of life, of thought, of salvation, of inner conviction and experience about man's relation to God as revealed through Jesus Christ. Through Christ, it was claimed, man's relationship to God was altered. Still a sinner, man would nevertheless receive and accept God's forgiveness, and would be a new creature. Men would then be humble, obedient, and joyful before God, as his nature and his love were revealed in Christ. They would be open to guidance in all their affairs by God's Holy Spirit (not, be it noted, by God's Holy Regulation). But precisely what this should mean in all the detailed relationships of life was not set forth in final form. The New Testament had no Blackstone or Marquis of Queensbury to indicate what the Christian gospel should imply for every detail of life, whether about sex or anything else. Because of this, equally devoted and conscientious groups of men have drawn differing implications.

Differences have also arisen because of different convictions about the source of authority in Christianity. Some, like the Roman Catholic Church, have held that such authority resides not only in the Bible, and in Christ revealed in the Bible, but also in the actual Church as the body of Christ on earth, and in the pope as the vicar of Christ. Close to the other extreme, some groups of Protestants have held that the sole authority is in the Bible in such a literal sense that if the Bible does not give warrant, for example, to the use of instrumental music in worship, then such music should be done away with. The view of the great Protestant Reformers was less literal and more basic—that the authority is Jesus Christ as revealed through the Bible, brought by the

Holy Spirit into the hearts of men, ordinarily through the medium of the visible fellowship or church. In so far as there have been differences about the source of Christian authority, equally conscientious Christians have tended to look in different places for the meaning and basis of Christian faith and life, whether in relation to sex or other things.

We may note also that Christianity is, and has always been considered by Christians to be, a *historical* religion. It is not solely a body of principles or truths, however important such principles and truths may be to it. Christianity emerged in actual events, Jesus as the Christ (the anointed of God) entering the world to redeem it. Christianity developed, in other words, from something concrete. But a "view of" something, such as sex, is never quite the same as something concrete. A "view of" takes what is basic in one situation and applies it to another situation. One can not transfer the whole concrete original to the new situation. In this translation process, from one concrete situation and one historical era to another, there may indeed be differences of implication among equally devoted Christians.

Christians have not been unaware that other Christians have held different views of the meaning of the faith. In the face of the diversity, some churches have simply declared themselves right and others wrong. Especially among the Protestant churches, and notably through the ecumenical movement of our own time, there has been the conviction that others too may have facets of the truth, and that both commonness and differences are worthy of continued exploration. From this point of view, each church is less than the full body of Christ, as each Christian is less than a completely successful follower of the will of God. Even together, they are less than the True Church of those who follow Christ. In constructive and critical co-operation with one another, however, they may be closer to the True Church than they would otherwise be.

Where the ecumenical spirit has prevailed, there is a method for dealing with differences of conviction. This does not eliminate differences, but it shows areas of agreement deeper than had been realized. And it provides a means and a motivation for subjecting one's own convictions to the judgment of others who, by the grace of God, may have light to shed upon them.

It is in such ecumenical spirit that this author's understanding of the Christian view of sex is presented. If there should creep into it any arrogance implying that any other interpretation of the Christian view is wholly wrong, the intention would be defeated. If, on the other hand, the impression should be given that anyone's view is as Christian as any other's, or that the differences are merely matters of taste, it would be leaning too far backward on basic convictions.

Whatever the variety of views about sex among Christians, there are much greater ranges of opinion among non-Christians. And since Christians do not live in a world sealed off from all except fellow Christians, these other views of sex must constantly be considered by Christians. Sometimes such views are openly stated, for instance, as various degrees of libertinism or of the renunciation of sexual behavior. When this is the case, it is comparatively easy, in the light of the Christian principles to be discussed in the chapters following, to come to terms with the views involved.

The differing views that are genuine dangers, however, meet us in another way—in the form of basic underlying attitudes, rarely if ever completely enunciated, but molding the views of sex, so to speak, from the inside. Studies by sociologists, by social psychologists, and by Kinsey suggest that these differing underlying attitudes, at least in our culture, are associated especially with different class groups in society, when class is thought of in such terms as formal education or its lack, mode of social relatedness to other people, and other similar factors of which income level may be one.

The important point seems to be that in different levels of our society, people are taught to take for granted certain things about their attitude toward sex, so that these taken-for-granted things ordinarily remain beyond examination. And the things taken for granted by one group may be those that appear most crude or unnatural to the other. For instance, relatively well-educated people seem usually indifferent about having their children glimpse them in the nude at home; whereas relatively uneducated people often regard it as unnatural to have nudity in the home even when sexual intercourse is being engaged in with the spouse. As another illustration, many boys from homes with a relatively low educational level regard masturbation as unnatural, and yet think of premarital sexual intercourse as a kind of compulsion rather than a right-or-wrong matter; while boys from homes of a relatively high educational level may assume that the one question about premarital intercourse is right-or-wrong, but may be morally indifferent to masturbation.

In another place I have tried to draw together the evidence pointing to the existence, in our own society, of six fundamental attitudes toward sex.[1] Although the evidence is not presented here, each of the attitudes will be mentioned in summary form.

The first of these is the *child-of-nature* attitude. This regards the pressure of sex for expression as natural, inevitable, and almost like a flood. To people who hold other attitudes, this seems simply crude, but it is not crude in intent. It oversimplifies sex and fails to link it with imagination. If its defect is in identifying sex only as a partial or segmental fact of life, its virtue is in its intention to make it a natural part of life characterized by expression rather than by restraint or withholding. This attitude seems to be declining in American society. In this form, it is impossible to be held except by persons of relatively little education.

The second is what can be called a *respectability-restraint* attitude. To the group holding this attitude, sex is a problem, or something to be feared, as it is not for the first-named group. To see sex as a problem is, for this group, a kind of badge showing that it has moved beyond the cruder levels of society. As naturalness was the criterion of the first group, so lack of respectability becomes the thing, above all else, that the second group wishes to avoid. Sex, therefore, becomes mainly something negative. The main thing to be said about sex is that it should be kept in its place. This attitude is in conflict within itself. The overemphasis on restraint suggests that the holders of this attitude secretly regard sex as a flood while openly asserting the opposite. The defect lies in the unwitting hypocrisy. The merit of the intention is the recognition that sex must be taken seriously. This attitude too seems to be declining in strength.

The attitude that is gaining most rapidly in strength in our society is what may be called *romantic*, when this term is understood in a specific way. This assumes that the most important thing is finding, now or later, the proper partner. There may indeed be sex problems other than this, but in the long run they are assumed to be of small import compared with finding the partner. Of course one does not assume that all of life and marriage will be dreamy and serene; but, together, the partners can work out their lives to mutual satisfaction, including their sex life. Such an attitude seems, in most instances, to work rather well in the earliest years of marriage, but to have its most severe trials ten or twenty years after the wedding.

In some respects this attitude lacks realism. It expects more from a partner than any human being can produce. It makes little allowance for the replacement of the exciting mutuality of early marriage by something deeper later on. Its virtues are of course considerable. It believes in mutuality and tries to effect it. It tries hard to get intensity and steadfastness together in the sex life, and it believes in real companionship between the partners. As this attitude is developing in our society, however, it becomes associated in high degree with egocentric feelings not so recognized by the partners, such as pride, jealousy, hostility, betrayal, or exploitation. Because of the dominant position it now occupies, it requires examination with special care.

Three other attitudes may be noted briefly, for each of them is held by only a relatively small group of people.

There is the sophisticated *no-harm* attitude, holding that anything about sex goes so long as it produces no harm—that is to say, no obvious harm. The sex partners must enter the engagement voluntarily and without coercion. Pregnancy and disease are eliminated by contraceptives, and nothing is done that is publicly offensive. Sex is a private affair so long as it is in good taste and not obviously harmful. This attitude is not without merit in its intention to make sex other than a matter of respectability and restraint. But to maintain itself, it must superficialize the meaning of sex in order to confine the "harm" idea to the obvious.

Then there is the *toleration* attitude, often held by people who apply the romantic attitude to themselves. Sophisticated, desiring to understand that others need to be understood and not merely condemned, they propose an understanding toleration of the sex life of others. Plainly the plea for understanding of others who may be unlike ourselves is wholly positive, needed by all of us. But the implication that the sex attitudes and behavior of other people are only matters of personal preference, of no particular interest to us or to the community, seems to deny certain basic dimensions in the nature of sex itself.

Fortunately there seems to be a sixth attitude that is gaining strength, which I have designated accurately but awkwardly as the *personal-interpersonal* attitude. Here a man begins from such basic interpersonal values as love, mutuality, seeking the good of another, finding one's true self rather than a pseudoself, and the like. He holds that sex is one important factor in human life, and that its emotional power makes it an important potential instrument for moving man and society toward the realization of such ends as love, peace, and amity. He examines not only the uses of sex that work against these ends, but also the non-uses of sex that could work for these ends but fail to do so. He does not expect more from a partner than a fallible human being can produce, nor, of himself, more giving than a human being is capable of. He prepares to have his attitude deepen and change character, so that middle life does not find him either disillusioned or denying disillusionment by affecting the role of the gay dog. He is neither legalistic nor libertarian. He accepts himself equally as a biological and a social being, but without having to conform to a particular pattern set by either one. He is not preoccupied with right and wrong as extraneous and imposed factors. He believes there is a rightness and wrongness in every situation that deserves consideration on its own merits.

This last attitude is most clearly in line with the Christian view of sex that will be developed in what follows. Yet it should be noted that no one in our society holds this attitude in pure form untinctured by other attitudes. It is an attitude that may be striven toward, that some may hold in some degree. But no one can so identify his own actual self with it as to avoid any feeling of kinship with one or more of the other attitudes.

No one of the other five attitudes, we hold, is entirely without merit. None of them can or should be condemned outright and in its totality in the name of a Christian view of sex. None may, however, rest immune from searching criticism directed to it by the Christian view. Yet if there is some merit in each, at least in terms of intention, then there is some point of contact within each attitude that the Christian view may touch. That there are such points of contact gives hope that the Christian view may have a transforming influence upon the sex life of every Christian, regardless of his class, education, sophistication, or sex, and beyond to the people of the entire community.

CHAPTER 2

Sex in the Bible

Since the Bible is the medium through which the revelation of God in Jesus Christ comes to us as the "Word" that "drives Christ" into our hearts, as Martin Luther put it, it is important that we be as clear as possible about the way in which sex is regarded in the Bible.

Modern biblical scholarship warns us immediately that we must accept the fact of differences. The Bible was written over a period of many centuries. Not only did social conditions change. There were also change and development in the conception of God and his relationship to man, and in what flowed from these about man's conduct and man's good.

Even the most casual reader of the Old Testament knows that it was at one time not considered displeasing to God for a man to have more than one wife or concubine. He may not realize, however, that adultery in the Old Testament related almost entirely to sex acts by married women rather than by married men, and that the divorce problem to which Jesus addressed himself was one in which men of his day could secure divorce from women on virtually no grounds at all. There are certainly differences within the Bible, not alone on details but also on some fairly basic matters.

In spite of these differences, the reader can understand the biblical view of sex only as he looks for threads which run throughout as well as for the undeniable differences. Several strands alter their meaning, and especially their depth, as the biblical account progresses. If he stated these in the most primitive form in which they appeared, he would be doing injustice to the Bible. But if, beneath the differences, he recognizes no kinship between late (for example, Pauline) and early (Genesis, for instance) interpretations, then he is failing to see the Bible as the account of man's increasing understanding of the nature of his personal relation to God and the consequent social relation to his fellow man.

In those parts of the Old Testament which reflect the historically earliest conceptions of the Hebrew people, we find a conception of sex like that of the "mana" of which the anthropologists speak—a kind of mysterious, external, and wholly supernatural force that invades human life and human beings for good or for ill.[1] Thus one's destiny, sexual and otherwise, is largely under the control of outside forces, frequently acting in what seems to be an arbitrary manner, and against the most demonic invasions of which one does well to erect barriers in the form of rituals, taboos, and sacrifices. Thus the Old Testament proscriptions focused around a menstruating woman are very much detailed.[2]

Scholars believe that in early Israel (pre-Exilic Judaism) there was temple prostitution, not as a degradation of sex (as is any prostitution today) but as a ritualistic means of sacrifice, linking the "holy" with the "mysterious," and sex with "holiness" as well as with "mystery."

This early conception of sex as mystery undergoes profound changes as the biblical account moves on. The crudity and primitivity disappear, but the notion of sex as mystery continues. Through sex one comes to "know" another, and thereby to know something of the secret of his own existence.[3] The use of the term "know" as a synonym for sexual intercourse is not a matter of delicacy. Through sex, one discovers something he can explore in no other way. He is a physical being; and through sex he discovers something of another being, and thus also of himself, that he had not, from the inside, "known" before. The riddle of his existence does not lie in the

stars. Through his physical existence he has
received a gift that transcends the physical
existence he shares with animals. How this
happens is a mystery. Sex is in some basic
sense sacramental, in that a spiritual gift has
emerged through a physical act.[4] Sex is not
apart from God. It is a part of God's
creation.

Such a conception is far indeed from the
early Hebrew conception of sex as mystery,
but there is a thread running through the
development. Consider what other views
this view prevented, from the very beginning. There could be no mere animalism of
sex. Willy-nilly, forces of mystery, un-
known on a purely biological level, were
involved. Similarly, such a view prevented
a spiritism. The Hebrews could not say that
God created the mind and the disembodied
spirit (as some of the Greeks said), but that
man's ideal existence would shuffle off such
things as sex in a physical sense. To say that
God created sex also said that he worked, in

some sense, through sex—even though there might be mystery as to precisely how.

Even from the beginning, sex as mystery and as sacrament was related to the Hebrew understanding of God as personal and righteous. This conception also underwent development. From one point of view, the Old Testament can be read as a series of legalistic creations (to appease a righteous God, or to demonstrate change of heart by the people in their attitude toward God), always broken up by the prophetic witness that recalled men to need for true repentance and not merely formal obedience. If God was a personal and righteous God, and men sinned against him and went astray like lost sheep, then no amount of formal or ritualistic obedience by men could bring them back. It was, said the great prophets, God's love which could restore men.[5] Only a righteous God could have a will for men, and only a loving God could help men come, despite failures, to follow that will.

These movements of thought in the Old Testament provided the developing theological base for increasingly profound insight into the nature of sex as mystery and as sacramental in nature.

When the prophets (and Jesus concerning the Pharisees) set forth their criticisms of the legalisms and ritualisms, they did not say that all law (or order or structure) should be done away with because it was something imposed from without.[6] They criticized legalisms for betraying the function of God's law. Laws had been dealt with as external impositions (or as appeasements). Actually, they said, God's law is, at the same time, the law of man's true being. Legalisms always forget this. As Paul Tillich says in our own time, "theonomy" (literally, God-law) does not contradict "autonomy" (literally, self-law), but is essential to its fulfillment.[7] Thus, God has created man as a sexual being. His sexuality is not reprehensible and not accidental. It is deep and mys-

terious; but he cannot follow God's will
about this aspect of his being if he ignores
sex, or flattens it, or makes it his whole being. In itself it is good. It is up to him to use
it as God intended, for the fulfillment of his
own true being.

By the time we reach the four Gospels,
there are two main aspects of Jesus' teaching that have special relevance for sex. The
first is illustrated in the statement that he
came not to destroy the law but to fulfill
it.[8] He seemed to have little sympathy for
those who, avoiding examination of the
basic purpose of God, looked to specific
laws and justified or condemned on such
bases. His teaching about the sinfulness of
one who looks on a woman with adultery in
his heart should be read in this light.[9] If a
man "lusts" after a woman, such a limited
perspective upon people has become so basic
a part of his character that he does not see
the whole person who is there. This is the
sin—the rejection of a personal relationship,

the *use* of another person (even symbolically) as if she were not a person or child of God.

The other teaching of Jesus especially relevant to sex says that although sex is good, it is not the most important thing in life. Seek ye first the kingdom of God, is the way in which the most important thing is usually stated by Jesus.[10] Some might be "eunuchs" for the sake of the kingdom, he said.[11] It is as if Jesus had said, in modern terms: Whatever is created by God is good; if it is such a value, seek it; but if your seeking it deters you from reaching toward the most important thing in life, then put it aside, temporarily or permanently.

When we consider Paul and the remainder of the New Testament, we need to recall that a profound change had taken place. To Paul, it was not he but Christ who lived in him.[12] A new era had come. Jesus' followers, the early church, were Christ's "body," and they now worked, as he had worked, that the kingdom might come. The old and ordinary era had not wholly disappeared, but in Christ there was a new world. The meaning of anything, therefore, including sex, was then not quite the same as it had been before. All was to be viewed in the light of its work for or against the kingdom.

In view of Paul's conception of Christ working in him, and of his belief in the imminent and literal end of the world, the amazing thing is that he did not become spiritistic about sex, and simply suggest that true Christians could forget it. He was much tempted to take such a position, not only about sex but about other things as well. Believing so fully that Christ had made all things new, it was not easy for him to see many others, even other Christians, hanging on to the wrong aspects of the old. Some of his most beautiful writings are those with a vision of the new, like the Corinthians chapter on love.[13] But he was too much a Jew, a Christian, and a realist to believe that actual human life could deal with the old era merely by ignoring it.

Such statements of Paul as that it is better to marry than to burn, or that the immoral cannot enter the kingdom, have often been discussed as if they came from a crusty old bachelor with a moralistic disposition and a busybody temperament.[14] Such an interpretation seriously misunderstands Paul. His condemnation, in various passages, of the "flesh" is not antisexual, for the "flesh" to him represented that kind of use of one's body and mind which served only partial or segmental ends.[15] The body, on the other hand, which is the temple of the Holy Spirit, he said, is where sex belongs.[16] This is another way of saying, mainly, that sex is inevitably, in human beings, a function of one's total being. To see or use it as if it were not, as if it were something set apart not affecting the rest of what we now call our personality, is to follow the "flesh." But man's body is not accidental to him. It is not just something imposed on him in this life from which he will be freed in the next. Indeed, as theologians like Reinhold Niebuhr have reminded us, the notion of the resurrection of the body is itself another way of saying that man is not conceivable as man, in this or any life, except as he is or has a body.[17] This realism of Christianity, coming directly out of its Jewish heritage, was one of its most distinctive features in its early years, quite in contrast to the Greek environment to which it soon spread.

Paul's longest statement about sex appears in the seventh chapter of I Corinthians. In speaking to the unmarried, Paul is careful to note, "I have no command of the Lord"; that is, his comment is merely his own observation.[18] If they marry, he says, this is no sin; but he notes, prudentially, that "those who marry will have worldly troubles, and I would spare you that."[19] The most astonishing thing in his letter is the way he deals with persons who are married to non-Christians.[20] If the unbeliever insists on a separation, Paul will approve; but if not, he recommends remaining together. This is not on prudential grounds, but because "the unbelieving husband is consecrated through his wife."[21] He adds, "Wife, how do you know whether you will save your husband?"[22] There is a strong implication here that sex itself may be an agent of God to the unbeliever which the believer should not lightly cast aside.

Although Paul said a good deal about sex, his total views on sex cannot be gained from his explicit comments on the subject. This is in part because of his literal conviction (in which we now know him to have been mistaken) of the imminent end of the world. In the chapter from which we have quoted, Paul wrote, "The appointed time has grown very short; from now on, let those who have wives live as though they had none."[23] In a metaphorical sense, time is always short to the Christian. But the difference between the metaphorical and the literal is great in a matter like this.

Paul's views on other things, perhaps especially on the meaning of human freedom, may therefore be more revealing concerning the underlying attitude on which a view of sex would have been based, had he not expected a literal imminent end of the world. As Luther later discovered, Paul's radical doctrine of freedom had very shortly been watered down by the early church. If one is really a Christian, if it is Christ who liveth in the man, then, as a new being in Christ, that man lives a life of liberty and of spontaneity.[24] He is free from the control of the "flesh," whatever segmental and partial ends would divert him from the true end, and equally free from the control of law, in the sense of having to conform to formal prescriptions.

As a new being in Christ, even man's impulses are transformed, so that they are holy and right, as God intended. Because men

are sinful, law is needed. But the Christian
is the freest man of all.[25] If one truly loves
God, he may do as he pleases; because what
he freely pleases to do is to follow the will
of God. The main thing of course that Paul
wanted to do was to demonstrate the spon-
taneous, uncoerced, unforced, unimposed
character of the whole Christian life. The
Christian is above the law because he is
beyond it. He is not, ordinarily, against it;
but in principle, if law stands in the way of
the Christian freedom to follow God's will,
then he would be against it. Paul was against
the inner divisiveness of men that makes law
necessary, and for the unity, in Christ, that
makes it possible to be free under God. For
this he was denounced, even in his own
time, as a libertine. But there is no reason to
think he excluded sexual dimensions from
this conception of human freedom, so long
only as it was in Christ.

From the second chapter of Genesis
through the remainder of the Bible, there is

reference to "one-flesh" union. The two shall become one flesh. The essential meaning of this, rightly noted by the Anglican author D. S. Bailey, is that it has a radical character, whether one is aware of this or not.[26] What takes place is an organic rather than an arithmetical kind of union. It is a serious matter, for good or for ill.

No doubt this "one-flesh union" idea, in the early life of the Hebrew people, was of the "mana" type. Bailey's discussion is illuminating in showing that the development of this idea within the Bible leads toward the conclusion "that in every case the character of the union will be determined by the character of its constitutive act."[27] In any case, something serious takes place. Whether this is for good or for ill depends on many factors. There may be "false, invalid" unions, or "defective" unions.[28] Authentic unions in "one flesh" occur, Bailey says rightly, through "intercourse following consent between a man and a woman who love one another and who act freely, deliberately, responsibly, and with the knowledge and approval of the community, and in so doing (whether they know it or not) conform to the Divine law."[29]

It may appear strange to the reader that this entire discussion of the biblical view and views of sex has not, up to this point, mentioned reproduction; for the idea is very widespread that Christianity "justifies" sex activity only when it has a reproductive end immediately in view. Whatever point there may be to such a notion, it is not that of any part of the Bible. The Bible is not against propagation of the species, or against responsible family life in which children may be reared. Texts such as "Be fruitful and multiply" are expressions of God's favor of his people in particular, and are testimonies to his creatorship in general.[30] But when Adam and Eve became "one flesh," they "were both naked, and were not ashamed."[31] The matter is never put in terms of a *justification* of sex (as if it were otherwise reprehensible) because it leads eventually to reproduction. A purely reproductive notion of the Christian view of sex is not possible if one takes seriously the biblical views on one-flesh union, on sex as mystery, on sex as the creation of God, on man's body as fundamental and not peripheral to his nature, and on the freedom of the Christian.

One of the serious modern students of sex from the biblical point of view, Otto A. Piper, draws certain implications from his understanding of that view with which we must emphatically disagree.[32] He has, however, some penetrating things to say about the biblical view, including this excellent summary of the unity within the biblical view:

Sex does not represent the animal side of man, nor that of mere nature as distinct from what is spiritual. Such a depreciation is in contradiction to the biblical view of man. God deals

with each of us as a unity; both physical and
spiritual life therefore have to serve his purposes with equal necessity. Our physical and
mental capacities alike are created to reflect
God's nature. Hence the real problem of Christian life is not to eradicate sex influence from
the higher realms of life; rather it is so to shape
and direct sex through the will of the heart
which has been sanctified by God, that, just as
is the case with every other human quality, it
helps to fulfill God's purposes.[33]

Piper's summary of the biblical view of
sex is also worth examination. He holds the
following five ideas to be fundamental:

1. In sexual intercourse two persons of different sex become joined in an indissoluble unity.
2. Sex is meaningful in itself, creating a
   specific kind of personal relationship. It
   does not require a justification by concomitant features, as, for instance, the
   possibility of propagation which it
   offers.

3. In sex life one attains knowledge of the inner secret of one's own physical being.
4. In love sustained by faith sex attains its consummation and perfection.
5. Sex life is necessary and good, but not absolutely essential for a full human life.[34]

Properly interpreted, these statements represent the Bible accurately. We should, however, be cautious in the way we interpret the "indissoluble unity," the nature of "personal relationship," the meaning of "specific kind" (which may yet be of miserable quality), the meaning of "consummation and perfection," and the sense in which (and for whom) sex may be "not absolutely essential." Piper's statement does not, for example, mention Paul's doctrine of Christian liberty, nor the point that the "radical" nature of sex may make for good or for ill. But it is clear that in the Bible, sex is regarded as created by God, that man's body is not peripheral to his nature, that the revelation of spirit through body is a mystery and a revelation of the depth of human life, that sex life itself is to the glory of God, and that a merely reproductive view of sex is not biblical.

According to the Bible, sex is no enemy of the Christian life but is, instead, one of its important ingredients.

CHAPTER 3

Sex in Christian History

As we have seen in the discussion of sex in the Bible, there were change and development in views of sex from the earlier to the later biblical times. A similar fact of change is evident throughout Christian history. Some of these developments, as it is now realized, actually went against the dominant trends in the biblical views. Others, from the present vantage point, were essential in order to fulfill the intent of the biblical view under new conditions, and in areas to which the Bible had not devoted specific attention.

In his excellent historical analysis of what he regards as positive developments in the Christian view of sex through the ages, Roland H. Bainton points to three main strands or aspects.[1] The first is what he describes as *sacramental*. He uses this as an over-all term for the content of the biblical view of sex. It includes the seriousness, the mystery, and, above all, the sense of God's working through the material for spiritual ends. This view was radically opposed to any conception of sex or of marriage as merely a convenience, or just a private affair, or solely an affair of state.

The next positive development in the Christian view, Bainton notes, was the emergence of a *romantic* notion of relation between the sexes, beginning with the medieval age of chivalry. At first this was a matter of the knight looking from afar at his lovely lady (who was married to someone else), desiring her but giving her up for the sake of romance. This led to actual sex unions outside marriage for romantic reasons, as described in Boccaccio and Chaucer. But it led later to the idea of romance within marriage that is such a dominant part of our current conception of marriage in the Western world.

The third positive development, as Bainton sees it, was the notion that marriage and sex in marriage are for purposes of *companionship*. That meant that companionship between the partners through the whole gamut of life's experiences becomes a normative consideration. As such, Bainton believes this view has developed only since the Renaissance and the Reformation. His implication is that a Christian view today requires a merger of the sacramental, the romantic, and the companionable or companionship views of sex and of marriage. The seeds of this trinity, he implies, were in the earliest Christian gospel. But the two last could not come to flower until later cultural development made it possible.

There were, however, throughout Christian history, other developments in views of sex than those noted by Bainton. Some of these, we now believe, departed, however unwittingly, from the bases of the biblical views with their emphasis on sex as God's creation, as good, as mystery, and as requiring no justification if used to the glory of God. By the fourth century of our era, the suppression of any sex life was considered by many Christians to be a positive good in itself, better pleasing to God than the married state. Although marriage was not held to be contrary to God's will, it was felt to be inferior to celibacy. Many church leaders after the third or fourth century, unlike those of the New Testament, held or implied that abstinence from sexual expression was itself a kind of road to salvation. This was, as the Protestant Reformers later pointed out bluntly, attempting to achieve salvation by a form of "works."

As Protestants see it, the Roman Catholic Church moved, during the Middle Ages, to a position that contradicted important aspects of the biblical view of sex. This was especially because of the way in which the Church became associated with Roman law, and a general legalistic mind-set that re-

sulted. The dominant view of the Roman
Catholic Church about sex, even today, has
been called a "social solidarity" view. According to this, in its earlier and cruder
form, sex was justified by marriage, and
marriage was to found families for state and
church. In its more refined and subtle forms,
it emphasized sex in marriage for purposes
of procreation and the subsequent needed
solidarity of family life, for the relief of
"concupiscence," and in modern times also,
for the promotion of love and companionship between the partners.[2]

Protestants, obviously, cannot be against
the "social solidarity" of the family. But a
justification of sex mainly by its service to
a social institution seems to Protestants to
move away from the essential biblical view
of sex as God-given, as designed to reveal
the person to himself and to another, and
to help penetrate the depth and the mystery
of life. The Roman Catholic view of sex
tends to say less about sex than about the

family as a social institution. Thus, Protestant interpreters feel that in spite of the detailed attention that many Roman Catholic moral theologians have given to sex matters, there is not a fundamental and clear-cut view of sex as such within that Church. Roman Catholics of course see such Protestant criticisms as signs of individualism, idealism, or "antinomianism" (being against any law to the point of anarchy). One's total Christian experience must be taken into account in such evaluations. No Protestant criticism, however, of the Roman Catholic position should fail to note the immense amount of understanding of the frailties and weaknesses of men and women that a vast multitude of priests have had down through the ages, and the consequent help given to suffering and torn individuals.

The Protestant Reformation attempted a kind of revolution, in the sexual realm of life as in many others.[3] Luther left the mon-

astery, and then married, specifically because he felt that the monastic vows and
state were contrary to the Bible. The motivation for this was not sexual, but was a
denial of the notion that any special merit
was attached to renouncing the sexual side
of one's humanness. Man's salvation could
not come by "works," even those works
that professed to give special merit in God's
eyes by the renunciation of sex and of family responsibilities. As Luther saw it, the
New Testament teaching about some becoming eunuchs for the sake of the kingdom might mean that chastity and bachelor-
hood were personally preferable for some
people (he thought the number very few).
What it could not mean was that these people were better than others in the eyes of
God. It was the merit or "works" notion
that Luther considered dominant in the
Roman Church of his time, and against
which he felt compelled to rebel.

To Luther all that God created was good.

But man's sin perverted it all, from top to bottom. There was no more sin in man's sex life than in his religious life. To think that the saying of prayers, or the refraining from sexual activity, could in themselves be agents of salvation was to misunderstand the total and organic nature of man's sin—sin being man's alienation from God and from what God intended him to be.

The true path of salvation, then, said Luther, was through "faith" not meritorious works. In faith one rested on God and his grace and mercy through Jesus Christ, and then acted, as a new Christian being, in the full freedom of which Paul had spoken. Man would continue to sin, but God's forgiveness would always be available. If one kept his eye on the main thing, that it was God's initiative through Christ that brought him forgiveness in faith, then the result would be a life of love and good works. But the good works would follow faith, and not be an illusory and deceptive instrument for avoiding the claims of faith.

What keeps man alienated from God is not his natural or biological nature. Instead, it is the action of his total being or spirit rebelling against God, or trying to appease God through legalisms or good works. As Luther saw it, there is nothing inherently sinful in sex from which a special justification or sanction is needed to free it. So he, along with the other leaders of the Reformation, held that marriage was not a sacrament. This was partly in order to make clear that there was no peculiar form of guilt inherent in sex from which freeing must be accomplished by special rites. The Reformers believed, however, that sex and marriage were sacramental in the sense that this realm of life, like other realms, might reveal the majesty and goodness of God through the things of common human experience.

There were other aspects of the views of Luther and his fellow Reformers that were less close to the biblical view, and closer to the Roman Catholic view, than they thought. Not a little of the social solidarity view was taken over intact, with the family as a social institution partly justifying sex by being a school for young Christians. Little was said about the mystery of sex. And in the desire to show that marriage was not a sacrament, they said too little about the sacramental meaning of sex and of marriage in the biblical sense.

They adopted the Roman notion of marriage as intended, in some part, for the relief of "concupiscence." Little was done by Luther and Calvin to domesticate the romantic aspect within sex and marriage. And it was to be some time before the companionship idea as normative would make its appearance. In Calvin especially, the response to the "mystery" aspect of sex tended to be in the form of a call for self-control even in marriage. It was this tone that set the stage for some later legalisms and coldness about sex in Protestantism, even though the dominant position of the Protestant Reformers was positive rather than negative in its thrust.

The later history of Protestant views of sex may be seen as something like a tug of war. On the one side there was the emergence of the romantic and the companionship aspects of sex relationships, to go hand in hand with the sacramental. But on the other side there was some tendency to be either cold-bloodedly rationalist; or through one of the many forms of Pietism, to retreat to a legalism or a "social solidarity" view. Right into our own time a marriage service, while still held in most of Protestantism to be not a sacrament (as a special act instituted by Jesus Christ), nevertheless has tended to become mainly an act of the church as a social institution giving its blessing. This is a "respectability" notion of the marriage ceremony, and it is too easily divorced from its religious roots. A marriage ceremony becomes institution-centered rather than God-centered.

Otto Piper holds that in later Protestantism,

> . . . the immorality of nonconjugal sexual intercourse was seen primarily in the fact that it lacked social sanction. . . . Therefore it was not the fact itself, but that it might become known, that made the nonconjugal form of sex life harmful. Virginity and chastity thus came to be matters of purely conventional value, apparently without a factual basis for their necessity.[4]

Although this is an extreme statement, there is some truth in it. The prudishness that made several generations of Protestant theologians discuss marriage with practically no direct reference to sex supports the notion that some aspects of later Protestantism distorted the biblical and the Reformation views of sex.

We should note also the tendency to avoid being specific about most matters of sex. In contrast, the Roman Catholic Church never spared its theologians in the construction of moral theologies which went into all possible details. In Christian sex ethics, Protestantism often resorted merely to general principle. While principle is basic, its relevance becomes clear only as it is explicitly associated with the materials of concrete living. In large measure, this task still remains to be done about sexual matters. But recent works on marriage, on birth control, on divorce, and on artificial insemination as partial aspects of the larger sex question have laid the groundwork for more forthright Christian statements on sex.

Close to our own time, and even now, we have witnessed some distortions of the Christian view of sex that are especially hard for us to recognize because they have been so much a part of our own backgrounds. These have tended to take two

forms, one for those who regarded themselves as more conservative, and another for
those who associated themselves with a liberal tradition.

The first group has tended to rest on a
kind of moralism suspecting sex itself of
being sinful, although "justified" by marriage. This has often meant that persons not
conforming entirely to the official attitudes
or patterns of conduct were automatically
excluded from the religious community.
Such a view accords neither with the
biblical view nor with that of the Protestant
Reformers. In practice, however uninten-
tionally, its consequences have sometimes
been cruel. The correction of it is not of
course any mere matter of saying that anything goes.

The liberal tradition of the generation
just passed, on the contrary, set about to
rediscover the meaning of marriage. Boldly
taking sex discussion out of the cellar, it
advocated sex as a foundation stone of

happy marriage, to be sought through right attitudes and some knowledge of techniques. Young people should get to know one another (nonsexually) before marriage, although the activities of sex should be reserved for the lifelong partner. Far from suppressing sex, more should be made of it, as an instrument to foster happy unions, which would in turn produce happy families, and out of which would come happy children for a new age in which the misuses of sex would fortunately diminish.

So far as such a statement goes, there is nothing in it that explicitly contradicts a Christian view, but it is astonishing how much of the Christian view it omits to mention, and how far the conclusion it implies is from the Christian conclusion. In this view there is little about sacrament and mystery in the Christian sense. By implication what counts is finding one's true partner, and happiness will flow from that. The avoidance of sex partners other than the spouse is mainly prudential. There is little reference to the radical and serious character of sex experience itself. Nothing in particular is said about the problems of living with a spouse or of sex in itself. Proper knowledge and technique are rather assumed to take care of all these problems.

Despite the conscious intention, this liberal-romantic view superficializes sex. In a sophisticated way sex is still contaminated rather than being something good created by God. What is needed to fumigate it is not a sacrament of a marriage service but a particular kind of subjective feeling usually called "love." If "love" is there, if there is the will to work out the sexual and marital destiny with the partner, and if there is appropriate knowledge of techniques (sexual, budgetary, or social), then the couple are likely to succeed.

Yet the fact is that they can fail, and many do. Besides, many other people will not marry. Homosexuals will continue to be produced by poor rearing. Masturbation will go on troubling youngsters even if they cease "worrying" about it. Sex crimes will still occur. Family quarreling will at times be anything but creative. To speak in this way is not fatalism but realism.

So far as possible, all such situations ought to be prevented and, if they occur, to be alleviated. No possible stone should be left unturned to prevent and to help. Man is still a sinful creature. It may be in his highest aspirations for his marriage, rather than in his weakest sexual moments, that he sins most grievously. Here pride, which he may not recognize, may produce his longest fall, which he may also fail to recognize. Happy after a fashion in his own marriage, he may totally lose sympathy for those who appear to have more problems than he acknowledges, or who offend against sex laws, or against the "romantic" code of decency.

There are good and healthy signs that sex in its many dimensions is being re-exam-

ined today in the light of Christian principles and Christian history. A competent
book like that of William Graham Cole sets
forth constructive Christian principles in
the light of Christian historical developments, and alleges that the basic findings
about sex in psychoanalysis are in accord
with the fundamental Christian view of
sex.[5]

Having traced briefly the views of sex in
the Bible and in Western Christian history,
we may proceed to a constructive restate-
ment of the Christian view of sex for today.
Such a statement of the place of sex in the
Christian life must not overlook the truths
contained in all aspects of the tradition, but
it must also subject all previous statements
to careful criticism. This is especially important in relation to the "liberal-romantic"
view because of its wide currency, whether
in religious or secular clothing, in our own
day.

Our review of views of sex in Christian

history makes it clear that there have been gains, and we do well to capitalize on these gains for our day. The achievements of the romantic and the companionship aspects of sex and marriage relationships are positive and important. But where these achievements threaten, as they sometimes do, to efface or dilute the basic sacramental view of the Bible—that God reveals himself radically and in mystery, and therefore reveals us to ourselves and to each other, through things of the common life like sex—then there have been losses that need to be examined and guarded against. Our statement will attempt to sustain the gains and get rid of the distortions and losses.

CHAPTER 4

A Modern Christian View

Here an attempt will be made to state a modern Christian view of the place of sex in the Christian life. This is based firmly in the biblical view, but it takes into account the modern knowledge symbolized by "developmental understanding," as well as the developments within Christian history since Bible times. As far as possible, the statements themselves are put in the language of the modern world as well as in the traditional language of Christian thought.

1. *Since man is a whole or total being, sex is good if it serves the fulfillment of man as a total being, that is, if it serves God's will for man.* As a whole or total being, a personal spirit, or a self-transcending organism, man is not essentially something ethereal with body temporarily attached.

Nor is he an animal with the misfortune of a lately-developed brain that complicates an otherwise simple biological existence. Sex for him is not an unhappy reminder of the link that binds him to an animal ancestry. Nor is sex for him more real or essential in its biological than in its psychological, social, or religious aspects.

Because man is a total personal spirit (including body), his sex life can never be merely animal in nature even when he tries to make it so. On the other hand, since man's body *is* man seen from one perspective, man's sex life is not something alien linked to an otherwise free being. God seeks the fulfillment and realization of his creatures according to his will for them, and so he blesses sex that it may be used toward that fulfillment. Man is neither animal nor angel in his essential nature, but personal spirit and self-transcending organism.

It is of the utmost importance to recognize that sex in the service of the will of

God does not refer to something alien or imposed. God's will simply provides the necessary objective reference, whose subjective counterpart is man's fulfillment as a total being. One of the reasons that the biblical and sacramental conception of sex has been so largely neglected in the modern world (that is, that something of the divine is communicated through biological experience) has been the unjustified suspicion that any reference to God means an unpleasant, external, and alien imposition. That is bad Christian theology.

Even the responsible humanistic views of sex today hold that sex is for man's fulfillment as a total being, rather than merely as a creature of biology, or a disembodied ghost, or as an unstable combination of the two. In its thrust, the Christian view does not, on the subjective side, differ in principle from the best humanistic views. It doubts, however, that the full dimensions of human fulfillment are likely to be kept in mind if the reference to God is omitted. Nevertheless, any recognition of sex as relevant to the total dimensions of man's existence, and not just to some segment of that existence, is implicitly in line with the Christian view. Conversely, any view that confines sex to one or another aspect of man's being, as if it were hermetically sealed off from other aspects and dimensions, is implicitly a contradiction or foreshortening of the Christian view.

2. *Man's total self or being (spiritual or organismic) has its very existence in the community of other selves; and it is the aim of all human interrelationships in all their aspects (including the sexual) to foster the love in which spiritual or organismic selfhood is nurtured.* It has never been an easy task for Christianity to find effective ways of stating that we are members one of another, that it is our "membership" in one another that is the source and, in some respects, the end of our selfhood. Many kinds

of metaphors and analogies have been used for this purpose. No man is an island, said John Donne. We are members of the body of Christ, said Paul. Our relationships to others are not merely external, as if we were what is inside our skin and other people were to us only as external environment.

Some modern tools, discoveries, and concepts have now come to our aid at this point. A "field theory" of personality is developing, according to which each man's individuality is real but is to be seen as the "focus" of a whole "field" or network of interrelationships. Without such a network or field, there could not be a focus. Focus and field are related internally and not merely accidentally.[1]

Our very selfhood is made up of "reflected appraisals" of other people in the course of our development, wrote George Herbert Mead.[2] It is equally essential to man as man that he express his "homonomous" needs (for relationship) as that he develop his "autonomous" ones (for personal expression and integrity), writes the psychiatrist, Andras Angyal.[3] These modern tools, insights, and concepts are genuinely original, and they provide a technical knowledge of the processes of personality formation never before available. They are immensely valuable in filling in the Christian conviction that men are members one of another.

Along with all other types of relationship, contact, and human expressiveness, sex too is to promote the love which is the matrix of human personality itself. Human living is inevitably a matter of relationship. In addition to acknowledging this fact, the Christian view immediately states that what counts about the relationship is its quality. The goal of all relationship is love in the Christian sense; and sexual relationships are no exception.

This interpersonal or members-one-of-another conception of human life is not, we should note, a swallowing up of personhood

or individuality in some collectivity. When
the relationships operate as intended by
God, they sharpen individuality. If it had
no such relationships, individuality would
be of poor quality, if it could exist at all.
There have sometimes been sentimental interpretations of the "one-flesh union" idea
found in the Bible, as if two persons becoming one cease to be individuals. This is not
the Christian insight. Perhaps peculiarly
with sex, one's personhood is "opened up,"
and individuality is accentuated. One looks
at all of life with a new look.

The Christian view is not sentimental or
unrealistic about the conflicts and discrepancies that are bound to arise between our
individuality and the interpersonal setting
in which it exists. Applied to sex, for instance, there is no guarantee, in the Christian view, that the choice of the best possible partner will solve all the needs and
wants of either individual who is involved.
Ultimately, Christianity traces most of these

discrepancies to man's sin. But such a recognition, while liberating, does not automatically change the character of individuality nor of relationships to bring them into a magical kind of romantic harmony.

Sexual relationships, like other relationships, constantly drive toward the realization of a love quality (although the person may be unaware of this). Yet there are always severe limits to the realization of this quality (although he may be unaware of this also). Thus sex, in a particular but not isolated way, always has a paradoxical element about it. Although he may try to deny it, the person receives something more from it than he had anticipated. It proves to be a gift transcending what he had deliberately set out to achieve. At the same time, even his best efforts to make it fulfill its high potentialities reach, inevitably, some level of frustration or alienation.

No one can find perfect peace by sinking into some "great All" of sexual relationship with another. Yet he who cannot "let go" and accept the gift transcending his expectations is not moving toward love at all. From the Christian point of view, man is a sinner. Yet God forgives him, and that forgiveness may be manifested in many ways, including the gift coming to him through sex of a kind and quality he had neither planned nor anticipated. The reception of this gift does not mean that individuality disappears, nor does it give complete release from the problems and even the isolation that inhere in the fact of individuality.

If the Christian view rests on our being members one of another, seeking that quality of relationship that is Christian love, but sharpening rather than qualifying our individuality, then it must be stated and interpreted developmentally if it is not to be just an "end-point morality" heedless of the stages by which human growth takes place. The little child does not learn the love quality of relationship at once but through very complicated stages of actual relationship. Many of these stages bear little resemblance, on the surface, to adult love. In addition, people may become "fixated," as Freud said, at various stages of such development. They may thus move into chronological adulthood with the base capacity for love greatly impaired.

Unless we understand something of what is going on within the person and his relationships (including the sexual), we are not in a position to know to what extent he is or is not moving in the direction of a love quality of relationships. With this insight, the Christian view thus entertains a kind of clinical caution without impairing its vision of the basic principle. If we ask when this or that person is so moving, the answer is difficult. In answering it, casual observations and snap judgments have no place.

3. *The developmental aim of sex in human life is toward a progressive integration of the several necessary levels of sexual pur-*

pose or function. Biologically speaking, sex reduces tension. Psychologically, through sex we find unsuspected aspects of our selfhood. Socially, we discover depth in another and, by implication, the potential depth of all other persons. Ethically, we find the relationship between fulfillment and responsibility. Theologically, we see sex ultimately as a mystery, but a mystery whose meaning is revealed to us in part.

Perhaps we can assume that to God, all these aspects or purposes of sex are one; for, from the Christian view, they are all necessary as aspects of the will of God for man in relation to sex. But since we are human, we come to comprehend them as if they were separate "things." Their meaning comes into our experience at different times and seasons. We are forever tempted to isolate one or more of them from the others, or to fail to accept the insight of a new level of apprehension lest it disturb the satisfactions of the old. But the *development* of human sex life, normatively speaking, is toward an increasing integration of these purposes and perspectives.

The end-point of this integration of sexual purposes may be relatively clear—a mature adult whose sexual life releases biological tensions, moves him toward depths of self-discovery, leads him toward ever-deeper love for his partner and beyond to the depth in every person, convinces him increasingly that personal fulfillment and social responsibility go hand in hand, and reveals to him the mystery of sex so that it is at the same time serious, radical, and joyful.

But who, a sinner, has ever wholly arrived there? And who is not, in fact, wrestling at any stage of his life with one or another aspect that is stoutly resisting appropriate integration? Who has not, at one time or another, confronted such severe obstacles, from within or without, that he has, at least temporarily, given up the battle? And who has not, on some occasion, tried so hard that his very effort made the goal elude him? Who has not felt at times that he had arrived—only to realize that he has been equating dependency with mutuality, or possession with fulfillment?

This is the sexual corollary of the fact that all men sin and fall short, but it is also more than that. It is a recognition that the Christian life, while lived with the end-point in view, is always an imperfect life in process of development. Though development cannot occur without some vision of its goal, a preoccupation with the goal at the expense of the next step in the process defeats the very chance of approaching the goal.

A previous chapter emphasized how deeply the biblical view regards sex as, ultimately, a mystery, that through biology there could emerge new dimensions and realizations of man as total spirit. This is profoundly true. However, if a Christian concentrated exclusively on sex as mystery, at the expense of its other legitimate dimensions and perspectives, he might well become so inhibited or so withdrawn as to be incapable of any sex life at all. An adolescent boy who thought only of the mystery of sex would have a difficult time on his date. He and his girl may engage in much casual banter; but this does not negate the fact of sex as serious business or as mystery. What actually takes place may lead developmentally toward the ultimate integration of the several purposes of sex in their lives.

In the metaphor used through the Christian ages, the Christian life is a "school" for everyone. Even if one is in the faith and has been "saved," he is still, in the language of the Reformers, a candidate for "sanctification." No man wholly arrives, becomes a "saint." The whole of the Christian life is to be a pupil, or a "pilgrim," moving toward a goal but aware that it has not been achieved and that one cannot, therefore, look down arrogantly on other men. The

vision of the goal is of great importance, but
it is not a substitute for the actual process of
development.

4. *In its human dimensions, sex requires
both intensity and steadfastness, and a
proper relationship between them.* We may
consider first intensity and then steadfastness, and finally the relationship between
them. That sex is presumed to have intensity
implies first that the attempt to make it
merely casual or flat would distort its inherent meaning. This means more than being
against that view of sex that sees it as a
"drink of water." It means also that sex
"with reservations" is equally a distortion.
In its inherent nature sex is radical and serious. If one acts sexually, but withholds in
one way or another, he is in effect denying
the radical and serious nature of sex. Flat-
ness, as well as casualness, works against the
intensity inherent in sex.

Intensity is desirable from each of the
relevant perspectives: biologically, in the

intense pleasure of the encounter and the orgasm; psychologically, in the discovery of unsuspected depths in the self; socially, in the depth of discovery of another; ethically, in the integration of fulfillment and responsibility; and theologically, in the deepening sense of the mystery. The arbitrary or permanent exclusion of any aspect of intensity foreshortens the meaning of sex.

Steadfastness is also desirable from each of these perspectives: biologically, in the form of physical fidelity to another; psychologically, in the sense of movement toward depth and not merely toward breadth or thrill; socially, in the constant recognition of new depth in the other and, by implication, in all other persons potentially; ethically, in the responsibility that, far from destroying fulfillment, goes along with it; and theologically, in the growing conviction that true faithfulness is its own reward.

But a merely flat, routine, and well-ordered but pleasureless sex life would be no more steadfast than it would be intense. If steadfastness meant only refraining from sex activity with persons other than a spouse, it might have some minimal value from the point of view of social order. That would be very far, however, from the Christian understanding of steadfastness in a full and positive sense. Steadfastness is not a negative but a very affirmative quality. It is distinguished by what it seeks, much more than by what it refrains from.

Implicit in the Christian view is the conviction that in their full human dimensions, intensity and steadfastness are likely to support and enhance each other. A movement toward full human intensity in sex will increase steadfastness; and a movement toward full human steadfastness will increase intensity. Therefore, these should be concomitant characteristics of the sex life. If there is one without the other, something is wrong. If one is so held as to exclude the other, something is still more wrong.

Developmentally speaking, the discovery of intensity and steadfastness in their full dimensions, and relating them appropriately, do not occur automatically. Very strong forces, both cultural and biological, attempt to prevent a union. A roustabout, orgasm-chasing, nothing-but-fun sex life may be wrongly represented to us as the most "intense." An anemic, unimaginative, full-of-restraint sex life may be wrongly held before us as the proper image of "fidelity." From the Christian view, both of these are caricatures. At the same time, it goes without saying that something other than condemnation is needed in relation to actual people who are not intense or steadfast or both.

5. *The meaning and the good of any sex act or relationship are always dependent, in some measure, upon the inner meaning to the persons involved; but the sole ultimate standard for meaning or good is the judgment and love of God, of which the Chris-*

tian community may at times be representative. This means, first, that no sex act can be judged entirely in and of itself, without some reference back to the character of the one who acts. A good tree bringeth forth good fruit, and a poor tree bringeth forth poor fruit. What the act means to the person is the index of his character. What appears, on superficial examination, to be the same act in one situation as in another, may not in fact be so if the character reference is made.

This statement means, second, that the ultimate good or ill of either an act or a character is impossible to know without reference to God, to that basic creating and supporting structure and power that indicates what it is in a man's character to become.

The third meaning is that the Christian community in its visible form is likely to have better ideas than most single individuals about what God's judgment and his love imply, but that there is no guarantee that this is so. According to Protestants, no visible manifestation of the church is itself without sin. The Protestant can never rest convinced that he is right merely because he does, or does not do, what his visible church tells him is right or wrong. Indeed, it is the readiness to bring everything, even the church, under the criticism of God's will that is the distinctive "Protestant principle," says Paul Tillich.

This last point is of great significance for the Christian view of sex. Again and again legalisms arise in which black-and-white definiteness is sought. Then all acts of Type A (regardless of their meaning to the person, the community, or God) are called wrong, and all acts of Type B (regardless of the same references) are called right. This situation invariably leads to more emphasis on calling wrong than on pronouncing right until, sometime, the pendulum swings, and libertinism in some form takes over.

The fact is that, however convenient it might be to pigeonhole sex acts, with no ambiguities or unclarities, this is very likely to do violence to the meanings and to the good that are involved. To be sure, some generalizations can be made, and are likely to be relevant to most situations of a similar type. But one cannot assume in advance that the mere external facts give him the necessary information about what is in the "heart."

This point implies further that if the good of any sex act rests in part upon its meaning to the person, there is a peculiarly human obligation for that person to consider the meaning of his act—to him as he is, to him as he wishes to become, and to God as he would find fulfillment through following God's will. From the Christian point of view, there can be no Christian morality that lacks reflectiveness about meaning. Man's mind and intelligence are true parts or aspects of him. To fail to use them is to foreshorten his self-discovery as a total human being. The Protestant view of sex demands, then, that the person's attitude be an "inner attitude," involving actual reflection on experience and decision about experience. There is no escape from a personal or "existential" decision to be—under God, but without an infallible guarantee of the extent to which one is acting according to God's will—a creator and molder of one's own character and selfhood.

Any community, church or otherwise, is likely to regard its own views on sex matters as being more right, or closer to the will of God, than those of any individual member. Against this tendency, which may indeed be oppressive and false, the Christian point may be interpreted as if the community had no stake in the matter. Actually the Christian view cannot deny the community's stake. But what it must do is to tell the community again and again that its attitude is as much under the judgment of God as is that of any individual. The mere fact of being a community does not make its judgment equal with the judgment of God.

We have attempted to set forth a Christian and Protestant view of sex in terms of general and inclusive principles, using modern language and concepts but referring back to the bases of the principles in the biblical view of sex. It may be that some unbiblical moderns will marvel at the modernity of the Bible. Biblically-minded readers may be surprised at how biblical some of the modern findings sound. In any event, it must be up to the reader to decide to what extent this modern synthesis does justice both to the biblical view and to modern knowledge.

CHAPTER 5

Some Practical Implications

QUESTION: If the attitudes that people actually have about sex fail to measure up to the Christian view, as you contend, does this not mean that the Christian view is out of date?

ANSWER: We may look at this first through an analogy. Suppose we ask: If all the efforts that have been made to prevent war have failed, does this not mean that peace is out of date? The answer to this is that peace is a positive value, whether or not we have succeeded in doing what is necessary to produce it. The fact of war is a commentary on the inadequacy of what we have done to prevent it, but it is not an indication that peace is undesirable or out of date.

The fact that existing attitudes toward sex all fail, in some way and degree, to fulfill the Christian view does not in itself say anything negative about the truth and value of the Christian view. The Christian view stands for certain values, that is, the kinds and qualities of relationship that should exist among men and between men and God. These are *ideal* values in the sense that they are the best we can conceive and in that we have not wholly realized them. But they are *real* values in the sense that man's deepest and most genuine potentialities come into being only as these values are, in some degree, made real. They are not ideal in the sense of being either irrelevant or unrealizable in any degree, just as they are not real in the sense that they are statistically dominant.

Some statements and some understandings of the Christian view *are* out of date.

When the statements fail to convey the real meaning, they do not perform their communicative function even though they may be technically correct. What is needed then is rethinking of their relevance to thought forms that will be meaningful to modern men and women. When the difficulty is not with statement, but with basic understanding of the nature of the Christian view, we are dealing not with something outdated but with a misapprehension of the Christian view itself.

QUESTION: If the Christian view of sex is so important for anyone who would live a Christian life, can it not be stated in a simple way so that any Christian can mold his attitudes by it?

ANSWER: Two kinds of answers are needed to this question. The first is that the essence of the Christian view *can* be stated simply. The second is that more is required than the essence of the view if it is to become incarnated as a personal attitude.

The essence of the Christian view is that sex is inevitably radical and serious, that it is a function of the whole human person including biology but also more, that it leads toward deeper self-discovery and to the awareness of greater depth in the other, and that it is a mystery since by it total spiritual meanings are conveyed through biological means. Put still more simply, the Christian view is that sex is the creation of God and is, therefore, good when used according to the will of God for life in human beings.

It is also true, however, that the distance between comprehending the simple core of the Christian view, and getting that view firmly rooted in our internal attitudes, may be great. This is because the core statement, to achieve simplicity, has relied partly on abstraction. Such a statement does not in itself tell us what, concretely, is the will of God for human beings. To discover that, we must study many things and not rely on a simple and abstract statement, however accurate. In addition, many forces and pressures in life work against the implications of the Christian view. Christianity does not deny the reality of evil nor its power. But we have contended that no existing attitude is wholly evil, that the Christian view can make some contact with every attitude, that there is some base in each from which to build in a Christian direction.

QUESTION: If it is so difficult to incorporate the Christian view into a personal attitude, do we not encourage hypocrisy by advocating it to people?

ANSWER: Provided a genuine Christian view is being advocated, where is the hypocrisy? The Christian view is not addressed to angels but to men and women, who sin and fall short, and who come to God through Christ to receive forgiveness and to be lifted again by God's grace. As some of the old theologians said, God forbid that this should mean, "Sin more that grace may much more abound." But the church is more a fellowship of repentant sinners than of triumphant saints. The crucial question is not whether one is a sinner (and falls short), but whether he is repentant. If he is, then he is not a hypocrite but a penitent.

We need to remember also that the Christian view is not a completely fixed code. It says we cannot separate the character of the act from the character of the person. Acts are hypocritical only when the person is hypocritical. This he cannot be if he truly hears the message. He may still be a sinner, and fail, but he is no hypocrite. The hypocrites are those who pretend to hear but do not, having what Kierkegaard called "shut-upness."

QUESTION: Is there any Christian standard about the amount and kind of sexual intercourse that married couples should have?

ANSWER: From the Christian point of view, that which promotes self-fulfillment of the partners, and mutuality between them, is good. If both partners felt these ends served by sex relationships every night, or once a month, the frequency would be appropriate in either instance. The real difficulty is likely to arise in different degrees of desire and interest on the part of the couple. Here it is true, as has often been said, that the man in particular should demonstrate tender concern for his wife, since she may not wish sex relations as often as he especially in the earlier years of marriage. On the other hand, clinical experience has taught us that one partner can be so preoccupied with the sexual feelings of the other that he loses his own spontaneity and therefore satisfies neither himself nor his partner. The Christian view rightly advocates true concern and love for the partner, but not at the expense of the intensity which one brings to the partner. Thus questions like frequency are both subtle and individual. In terms of *numbers* as such, there is no Christian standard.

In regard to the *forms* of sexual stimulation among married couples, there is also the joint criterion of self-fulfillment and fulfillment of the other. No form of such stimulation prior to coitus is wrong from the Christian point of view if both partners desire it and if it does not involve the personality-injuring cruelties of sadism or masochism. The intensity proper to a marriage relationship is likely to be aided by some novelty, whether this be in the sexual play prior to intercourse or the form of the intercourse itself.

QUESTION: Is it not true that the Christian view must always and invariably be against extramarital sex relations, because of the harm they do to the marriage?

ANSWER: There are really two questions here. The first is whether extramarital relations are wrong under all circumstances. Unless the circumstances are unusual, it is certainly true that the Christian view is against such relationships. It is important, however, to be clear about the basis of this disapproval. It is not primarily (as it tends rightly to be in the law) for the protection of the family as a social institution, although plainly that is important too. The basis for Christian disapproval lies in the fact that extramarital relations contradict the steadfastness that the Christian view sees as properly linked with intensity and depth. When there is such linkage, then there is personal and interpersonal humanization of sex. When steadfastness and intensity are divorced, something basic is lost. Most extramarital relationships clearly go straight against this conception of sex.

There may, however, be instances of extramarital relations in which the context ought to be examined with great care. A lonely soldier overseas, or his lonely wife back home, may be drawn into some sexual experience of which he or she truly repents and which would never have occurred without the enforced separation. A cold or bit-

ter wife or husband of middle years may
deny sex relationships to the partner, at the
same time denying the possibility of separation. Even in instances of this kind, though
the Christian view can hardly give approval
to such relationships, it must be cautious in
judging such instances. Their meaning may
be different in different circumstances. Often their existence may be a symptom of
deeper psychological or spiritual conflict
within.

The second part of the question implies
that the reason the Christian view is disap-
proving of extramarital relations is the
threat to the marriage. In principle, a comment has already been made on this. The
marriage itself is important. But in the last
analysis, marriage exists for persons rather
than persons for marriage. The deepest case
against extramarital relations lies in the in-
jury that may be done to persons (whether
the partners themselves, or the children)

rather than in the disorder that may result in marriage as a social institution.

QUESTION: If all married couples held the Christian view of sex in its proper form, would serious marriage conflicts be eliminated?

ANSWER: This is a very important question, and a difficult one to answer. In one sense, the answer is yes. If every married person not only held the Christian view of sex, but also had internalized it so that it was part of his basic attitude toward life, then it would follow that there would always be a basis of respect and love for the other person in which conflicts could be considered. And when conflicts can be considered in such an atmosphere, they are rarely serious in the sense of threatening to break up the structure of personality.

Yet, even in such fortunate circumstances, marriage would not be without conflicts. If a couple did not both have a Christian attitude toward economic standards of living, for instance, they might quarrel seriously over those standards even though their attitudes toward sex were closer to the Christian view. Of course the fact is that a full internalization of the Christian view of sex is possible only as there is, at the same time, an internalization of the Christian view of other things as well. One does not follow automatically from the others, even though they are intimately related.

But, even in the realm of sex itself, holding the Christian view is not likely to be a kind of insurance policy that eliminates all possible conflicts. Owing to reasons biological, psychological, or social, the partners may have quite different patterns of interest in relation to sex activity. Provided the whole Christian view of sex is in the minds and feelings of both partners, few such conflicts are likely to be insoluble. Neither are they likely to be solved easily or automatically.

QUESTION: Must we assume that premarital intercourse on the part of unmarried people is always wrong in the light of the Christian view of sex?

ANSWER: In principle, the Christian view of sex gives a negative answer to what is usually meant by premarital intercourse, that is, to a relation of such limited giving and receiving, personal and interpersonal responsibility, that the actual nature of sex in human life is thereby distorted. Not every act that is, technically, premarital intercourse (in the sense of pre-wedding) is of this nature, however.

Especially young people, being human, would like a clear and simple yes or no on this question, to which they might conform or against which they might rebel. Like the rest of us, they tend to resist honest analysis of the complex factors involved and the consequent unmistakably personal character of the decision for good or for ill. But yes or no can never be a substitute for this process of examination and personal decision. Everyone, regardless of what he decides, is going to make some mistakes, about sex or anything else. The critical question is whether he learns from them, and is open to correct and deepen himself as a result. No legalism and no libertinism will help him to do this.

Certainly there is a very real difference between the intercourse engaged in by a couple shortly before marriage, and the promiscuous intercourse engaged in by Don Juans or their female equivalents. In the latter instances, sex becomes simply the instrument of an exploitative ego structure, not the vehicle for mutuality and self-discovery in the truly personal sense. In the former case, the couple may be unwise for many kinds of reasons. They may thus inflate the importance of sex within marriage beyond its true proportions, and invite early disillusionment. Yet we recall the biblical concept of "one-flesh union." That union is sacramental, whether they realize it or not. In such a sense, the union marries them. The question then becomes social and psychological: if married in fact, why not bring the fact before the community?

QUESTION: Is there not a real difference between premarital intercourse and petting, even heavy petting?

ANSWER: There are certainly real differences between intercourse and even the heaviest petting. In the latter, the possibility of pregnancy is eliminated, the dangers of venereal disease infection are minimized, and it may be easier to provide the setting and arrangements. The preference for heavy petting with orgasm to coitus among some groups, however, seems due only in part to these factors. It seems to come also from the kind of value attached by these groups to virginity as a symbol. Technical virginity is maintained by a woman if the genital of the male has not entered her genital organs. One may wonder, however, whether the insistence on a technical definition of virginity seems legalistic and partly irrational. But one can not deny the difference in the rational factors especially in relation to pregnancy.

It should be noted that the Christian view implies something from the other side of the picture: What about the person who never has or expresses desires to caress or pet anyone of the opposite sex? This is likely to mean that there is a denial to oneself of one's own sexual nature. To be sure, bounds must be set and channels cut in terms of expression, as dictated by the fact of the radical and serious nature of sex experience in its full sense. But there is nothing in the Christian view to put a blanket "No" over those forms of petting among young people that do lead toward the Christian objectives. But let it be noted that the motives for much milder petting, as well as for sexual activity, often have little to do with sex. The boy who wants to prove himself virile, and the girl who wants assurance that she is popular, are using petting to support the ego rather than for purposes of sex-discovery in its Christian dimensions.

QUESTION: But since many young people seem to be engaged in premarital intercourse or in heavy petting, without any obvious harm resulting, is not one justified in going ahead?

ANSWER: That little word "justified" in the question is intriguing. According to the Christian view, sex itself requires no special justification. The question is whether sex is being used to fulfill its basic purposes in human life. This leads to questions of partner, motive, depth, and responsibility. But in none of these is the justification of sex the issue.

Suppose we rephrase the question so as to include at least some of the facts that are actually involved but not stated above. If a man and a woman accept sex as one dimension of their total human interrelationship, including its radical and serious character, and are prepared to follow through on all the personal, interpersonal, and social consequences of their association including the sexual, are they justified in going ahead with premarital intercourse or heavy petting? This certainly alters the original question. And if the original question did not imply what the second question states, then its concern is about considering sex in a less than radical way, with interpersonal relations strictly limited, with merely prudential social considerations, and with both intensity and steadfastness foreshortened.

QUESTION: Suppose that a young man or woman has begun to get out of the youthful class and, because of unattractiveness, illness, or similar reasons neither has married nor has any expectations of marriage. Does Christianity simply say he or she should have no sex life?

ANSWER: Traditionally, that is the answer most Christians have given. Although

there is wisdom and prudence behind such
an answer, it must appear abrupt to many
such people indicating a failure to understand the peculiarities and circumstances of
their situation. We recall that the Christian
view holds that sex is inherently radical and
serious in nature, whether people know this
or not. Therefore, it is unable to approve
sexual activity that rests upon merely casual
or nonserious premises. Because of the inherently radical character of sex, people
such as those indicated in this question
could not secure approval of relationships
which are clearly limited in some way that
prevents sex from being itself (in time, in
affection, or in other ways). Sex itself might
break these limits unpredictably at any time.
It is this that must be considered most seriously, more than the legal fact of no marriage.

If the question is pressed concerning the
unmarried man or woman with "honorable"
intentions who, nevertheless, cannot find a

partner of equally "honorable" intentions, then the answer is not simple. Nor is it a small problem numerically—for instance, in the war-torn countries of Europe where women considerably outnumber men. Against any possible libertine answer, the Christian view must simply testify to the radical and serious and, therefore, partly unpredictable nature of sex. But against a legalism that would simply condemn all sexual relationships of such people, regardless of context and motive, the Christian view would raise a warning. The general question would be: Under some conditions, may sex limited be better than no sex, provided the radical and serious character of sex is not denied? We need some ethical wrestling with this question.

QUESTION: What does the Christian view say to teen-agers about masturbation?

ANSWER: One is tempted to reply: Say as little as possible unless it becomes a compulsive habit injuring interpersonal relationships and inner self-development. That, however, would be not quite accurate. Attitudes toward masturbation differ sharply among different groups in our society. Among the less-educated groups, masturbation among boys, if it occurs at all, tends to be replaced very shortly by premarital intercourse. Among boys from college families, masturbation often continues until marriage and, on occasions, throughout married life. In order to have relevance, the Christian view must speak to the two or more types of attitudes involved.

Modern knowledge has taught us two things about masturbation. First, it may be a brief and, though troublesome, not unnatural aspect of self-discovery in adolescence, increasingly found unsatisfactory and abandoned because the very social essence of sex is absent from it. Second, masturbation may become compulsive, and thus a symptom of inner disorder not only in the sex life in the narrower sense but also in the total-relatedness character of life. In neither situation will help be given by mere condemnation. In the latter instance, what is needed is therapy to get at the underlying problems. In the former, either the situation will take care of itself; or understanding can help to distinguish between the nature of the impulse and its expression. We do not appropriately tell such people not to worry about it. We help them to find out the source of the worry, and to deal forthrightly with that.

QUESTION: May we assume that the Christian view of sex is plainly against homosexuality in any form?

ANSWER: It is certainly a presupposition of the Christian view that God created us male and female, and that the completion of each is assumed to rest in union with the other who is, in many basic respects, unlike himself. It is for this reason, more than for anything involving reproduction, that homosexuality in any kind of normative sense is disapproved by the Christian view.

But the total problem of homosexuality is not disposed of by such a statement. For one reason, many people discover themselves to have homosexual impulses, and seriously desire to alter this fact. Every possible therapeutic resource should be made available to them. When the desire to get help and to change is serious, even our present-day knowledge can do much for these people, and technical knowledge is expanding. A mere condemnation of such persons would be radically unchristian.

There are also persons with homosexual impulses who are so compulsive that at times, and against the "will" they are usually able to exercise, they become involved in overt behavior. Many of these people are not "fixed homosexuals" in the sense that they have inwardly accepted this form of behavior. It is just those people who are often caught and made to experience a kind of legal or other public degradation that makes their problem worse rather than better. They need therapeutic help, and so far too little of it is available.

Among the people who are "fixed homosexuals," without serious desire to alter their main condition, we need also to make distinctions. Some deal only with others of their own kind; others are predatory. Surely there are real differences here. We need to keep in mind that a fixed homosexual person is much more likely than a heterosexual person to have sex become the preoccupying center of his life. In larger cities this tends to create homosexual communities. There are very large social problems here for which no society has yet found anything like a tolerable answer. The Christian view cannot approve fixed homosexuality in any possible kind of normative sense. For those unamenable, however, to the possible change of their condition, neither condemnation nor passive acceptance of the condition seems adequate either. Only now has it become possible to discuss such a problem openly with the aim of analyzing the implications for it of the Christian view.

QUESTION: You have asserted that sex has a positive place in the Christian life. Does this mean that people who, for good reason, do not engage in sexual behavior cannot live a full Christian life?

ANSWER: If the whole question is considered, the flat answer is "No." People who, for good reason, do not engage in overt sexual behavior and relationships, can live a full Christian life, and many do. Protestants, with a married ministry, ought never, for instance, to imply that the celibacy of Roman Catholic priests and nuns is abnormal or a mark of deficiency in the full Christian life. For reasons like this that are inherent in the situation, or for individual reasons, many persons become very full and productive human beings, with their lives deeply related to the lives of others, and yet without overt sexual relationships of any kind. These people, whether from commitment or necessity, miss something significant in the gamut of potential life experience, as they are the first to say. But sex in terms of overt behavior is not the most important thing in life. Indeed, sex as overt behavior is not the basic thing about sex.

Whether from commitment or necessity, a person renouncing overt sex behavior does not thereby make himself or herself sexless. The main issue, of accepting one's own sexuality, must still be faced. Even if there is no sex behavior in the form of genital relationship, sex feelings are still inevitably involved in one's social and personal relationships with other people. As this is true for married persons in contacts outside the marriage relationship, so it is true for those without overt sexual relationship. The key lies in the inner acceptance of one's sexuality, so that even in essentially nonsexual relationships this fosters understanding and love in social and personal relationships.

Beginning with Luther, Protestants have rejected the notion that celibacy is superior in God's eyes. Thus Protestants deny that for most people, the abstinence from sexual relationship contributes to living a fuller Christian life. This is not, however, a negation of ability to live a full Christian life on the part of those for whom celibacy is either a personal misfortune or the result of a vocational commitment.

References

CHAPTER 1

1. *Sex Ethics and the Kinsey Reports* (New York: Association Press, 1953), Chapters 8 and 9.

CHAPTER 2

1. See, e.g., I Samuel 21:1-6 and Exodus 4:24-26.
2. Leviticus 12, and Leviticus 15:19-30.
3. See, e.g., Genesis 4:17, 25.
4. See Genesis 2:18-25, and The Song of Solomon in its entirety.
5. See Isaiah 40ff.
6. See Matthew 5:17.
7. *The Protestant Era* (Chicago: The University of Chicago Press, 1948), Chapter 4.
8. Matthew 5:17.
9. Matthew 5:27-30.
10. Luke 12:31.
11. Matthew 19:12.
12. Galatians 2:30.
13. I Corinthians 13.
14. I Corinthians 7:9 and Galatians 5:19-21.
15. See, especially, Galatians 5 and Romans 7.
16. See I Corinthians 6, especially verse 19.

123

17. *Faith and History* (New York: Charles Scribner's Sons, 1949), p. 149.
18. I Corinthians 7:25.
19. *Ibid.* 7:28.
20. *Ibid.* 7:12-16.
21. *Ibid.* 7:14.
22. *Ibid.* 7:16.
23. *Ibid.* 7:29.
24. See Romans, especially Chapters 1-8.
25. I Corinthians 7:22.
26. *The Mystery of Love and Marriage* (New York: Harper & Brothers, 1952).
27. *Ibid.*, p. 52.
28. *Ibid.*
29. *Ibid.*
30. Genesis 1:22.
31. Genesis 2:25.
32. *The Christian Interpretation of Sex* (New York: Charles Scribner's Sons, 1941).
33. *Ibid.*, pp. 105-106.
34. *Ibid.*, p. 30.

CHAPTER 3

1. *What Christianity Says About Sex, Love, and Marriage* (New York: Association Press, Reflection Books, 1957).
2. For a competent Protestant summary of the Roman Catholic view today see William Graham Cole, *Sex in Christianity and Psychoanalysis* (New York: Oxford University Press, 1955), Chapter 5.

3. *Ibid.*, Chapter 4.
4. Piper, *Op. Cit.*, p. 26.
5. Cole, *Op. Cit.*

CHAPTER 4

1. Gardner Murphy, *Personality: A Biosocial Approach to Origins and Structure* (New York: Harper & Brothers, 1947).
2. *Mind, Self and Society* (Chicago: The University of Chicago Press, 1934).
3. *Foundations for a Science of Personality* (New York: The Commonwealth Fund, 1941).

For Further Reading

Derrick Sherwin Bailey, *The Mystery of Love and Marriage* (New York: Harper & Brothers, 1952, 145 pp.). Very good exposition of the meaning of one-flesh union.

Roland H. Bainton, *What Christianity Says About Sex, Love, and Marriage* (New York: Association Press, Reflection Books, 1957, 124 pp.) Historical statement of the positive aspects of development in the Christian view.

Peter A. Bertocci, *The Human Venture in Sex, Love, and Marriage* (New York: Association Press, Haddam House, 1950, 143 pp.). Effective account of the Christian view of sex by a Christian philosopher.

William Graham Cole, *Sex in Christianity and Psychoanalysis* (New York: Oxford University Press, 1955, 329 pp.). The most comprehensive account available of the historical development of the Christian view of sex, along with an effective constructive statement.

Simon Doniger, Editor, *Sex and Religion Today* (New York: Association Press, 1953, 238 pp.). A thoughtful symposium by several ministers, psychiatrists, and others.

Sylvanus M. Duvall, *Men, Women and Morals* (New York: Association Press, 1952, 336 pp.). Contends that modern scientific study tends, in the main, to reinforce the conclusions derived from Christian morality.

Joseph Fletcher, *Morals and Medicine* (Princeton: Princeton University Press, 1954, 243 pp.). The most effective modern defense of a Protestant Christian position on contraception, artificial insemination, and sterilization.

Abraham N. Franzblau, *The Road to Sexual Maturity* (New York: Simon and Schuster, 1954, 280 pp.). An effective statement of the mutual reinforcement between psychiatric and psychoanalytic experience and the western moral tradition, by a psychiatrist who is also a professional in Jewish religious education.

George W. Henry, *All the Sexes* (New York: Rinehart and Company, 1955, 599 pp.). A comprehensive volume interpreting the varieties of sexual feeling and expression, by our greatest psychiatric authority on these matters.

Seward Hiltner, *Sex Ethics and the Kinsey Reports* (New York: Association Press, 1953, 238 pp.). Detailed evaluation of the findings of the first two Kinsey reports in the light of the Christian view of sex.

Jerome Himelhoch and Sylvia F. Fava, *Sexual Behavior in American Society* (New York: W. W. Norton & Company, 1955, 446 pp.). The best symposium analysis of the first two Kinsey studies, prepared by the Society for the Study of Social Problems.

Clarence Leuba, *Ethics in Sex Conduct* (New York: Association Press, 1948, 164 pp.). Addressed especially to young people.